Arlinda M. Garrett

~

I0087318

THINGS

THAT

MADEA

SAID...

An Amazon Trade Paperback

Things That Madea Said..
An Amazon Trade Paperback
Publishing History
Amazon Trade Paperback Edition/April 2015

Published by
DBA On-Demand Publishing
An Amazon Company
North Charleston, SC

Manufactured in the United States of America
First Edition

ISBN 10: 0692248560
ISBN 13: 9780692248560

Dedication

For my mother, the "*real*" MADEA...
Mildred Means
Being raised by my mother, a real-life
Madea, I learned life's lessons early. She
taught me the importance of keeping your
word (promise). I learned how to "stretch
a dollar and make it holla"
I remember thinking the "things that
Madea say must be something all people
say". It wasn't until I would casually
repeat the things I had heard--only to be
told that's some funny shit. Where did you
get that? It was then that I realized these
sayings are things only Madea would say.

Prologue

Live, Laugh, Love is the blue print for my life.

Laughter-eases the mind, body, and soul.

Love-is essential for the sustaining of the mind, body and soul.

Live-you can't live if you can't laugh. You can't laugh if you can't love

- Black people have the signs, white people have the money

- If your left hand itch, it's a sign that a letter is coming, if your right hand itch, it's a sign that money is coming. If both hands itch the money is coming in the mail

- A hit dog barks the loudest

- The squeaky wheel gets the oil

- A closed mouth don't get fed

- Mark it in the sand and let the rain settle it

- Put it in a Peace Pipe and smoke it

- Crazy don't mean LIAR

- Old enough to know better; young enough to try it again

- You don't have a pot to piss in, or a window to throw it out

- That is some BULL

- What you Eat Don't Make Me SHIT

- Looks like inmates running the prison

- Hee - Hee Hell!!

- You must stand for something or fall for anything

- As long as I owe you, you will never be broke

- Lack of planning on your part doesn't create an emergency on mine

- Those same shoes you got mad in, you'll get glad in

- Common sense ain't so common now-a-days

- A hard head makes a soft ass

- Don't Eat where you Shit

- It don't take all day to do nothing

- Go big or go home

- Go hard in the paint

- *Don't believe your lying eyes*

- *Don't PISS on me and tell me it's raining*

- *Don't dislike me, get like me*

- *Study long study wrong*

- *Drop your book, lose your lesson*

- *No Pain No Gain*

- *One monkey don't stop no show*

- There are four types of people: Willing and able. Unwilling and able. Willing and unable. Unwilling and unable.

- I'll beat the Black off you

- Momma's baby...... Daddy's maybe

- You can't see the picture when you're in the frame

- If you show up, GOD will show out

- We down like four flat tires

- Pump your breaks

- Best thing since sliced bread

- I figured that

- Be Gone, Poof!

- You are as dumb as a box of rocks

- You can't teach an old dog new tricks

- Sike!!!

- *Nigga pleaze!*

- *Don't Beat A Dead Horse*

- *No News is Good News*

- *I'm not new to it, I grew to it*

- *Fake It Till You Make It*

- *The game is to be sold not told*

- *The pot can't call the kettle black*

- You jumping out the pot into the fire

- There's more than one way to skin a cat

- A penny saved is a penny earned

- Scared money can't make money

- It's easier to ask for forgiveness than to ask for permission.

- Act like a duck and let it roll off your back

- The truth will make you fighting mad or fighting glad

- Keep your panties up and your dress down and everything will be alright

- Happy wife, happy life

- Free help ain't always good help

- Can't be friends with people who are jealous of you

- It ain't how much you make, It's how much you save

- When you're the smartest person in your circle of friends, it's time for a new circle.

- A nigga will fix his mouth to say anything

- You stuck on stupid

- J.O.B.= Just Over Broke

- Just like 2 peas in a bucket, F*CK IT

- Tell the truth and shame the devil

- You smelling yourself

- An honest day's pay for an honest day's work

- See what had happened, WAS

- GOD willing the creek don't rise

- Don't bite off more than you can chew

- Stretch a DOLLAR make it HOLLA

- So hung over you were praying to the porcelain God

- A fool and his money will soon part

- It ain't what you know; it's who you know

- That's just my Baby Daddy

- Who you know gets you there; What you know will keep you there

- Money out of sight starts a fight

- Don't put the CART before the horse

- If you bring some, you will get some

- KICK ROCKS

- Some money BEATS no money

- Ain't nothing slick to a can of oil

- It ain't nothing to a BOSS

- A minor setback for a major come back

- It's mind over matter, if you don't mind it don't matter

- If you don't have something good to say, DONT SAY NOTHIN

- Your eyes are bigger than your stomach

- Talk to the hand

- Fair exchange is no robbery

- Don't get your panties in a bunch

- Don't write a check your ass cant cash

- You can't turn a hoe into a house wife

- An even swap ain't no swindle

- If you can't stand the heat get out the kitchen

- If you can't hang with the big dogs then stay on the porch

- Don't try to reinvent the wheel, its already rolling just hop on and go

- Don't loan money you can't afford to give away

- Let Go and let GOD

- *Mean what you say; say what you mean*

- *Never trust a man who says trust me*

- *A broke clock it right two times a day*

- *No rest for the weary*

- *Never break more than 1 law at a time*

- You can bitch and moan or you can keep it moving

- Men lie, women lie, numbers don't; do the math

- Apples don't fall far from the tree; they fall right beneath it

- Keep your word because at the end of the day that's all you have

- What goes around comes around

- Good things come to those who wait

- Look up and read

- You can lead a horse to the water but you can't make him drink

- You're a liar and the truth ain't in you

- Scratch a liar and find a thief

- Niggas always trying to get popular off some bullshit

- Kill Yourself

- Hope I see you on the first 48

- When preparation meets opportunity it equals success

- Wish a nigga would

- Go pick a big switch

- Don't throw rocks if you live in a glass house.

Acknowledgement

First I would like give honor to God through him all things are possible.

I would also like to show my deepest appreciation to my friends and family for their unwavering love and support. Without you I wouldn't have a reason to continue this journey.

I Love You All

www.ingramcontent.com/pod-product-compliance
Lightning Source LLC
Chambersburg PA
CBHW071449040426
42445CB00012BA/1504